# MACRAMÉ FOR

# BEGINNERS:

A STEP-BY-STEP GUIDE FOR BEGINNERS TO MAKE
UNIQUE AND EASY MACRAMÉ. DETAILED &
ILLUSTRATED PROJECTS TO CREATE HANDMADE
OBJECTS FOR YOUR HOME & GARDEN DÉCOR.

**AMANDA KIM**

# © Copyright 2020 - All rights reserved.

# TABLE OF CONTENTS

# Introduction

For Men and Women Who'd like to Grasp How-to Macramé, There's a range of areas available on the marketplace. Creating intricate knots that produce whole patterns that could likewise be transformed to exquisite bracelets, flower baskets and decorative wall-hangings is just what Macramé is based on being a art. The exact first and elaborate step in looking to understand just how exactly to Macramé, at case that you're interested in this subject, is understanding how the basic knots and a couple of diagrams.

Visual skills are of immense Assistance and certainly will create Learning just how-to Macramé hassle-free. For a lot of people, it's a fantastic deal simpler to follow along with diagrams in the place of written guidelines which may be quite tricky to comprehend. Whenever you've familiarized yourself using the visual assistance, it's the perfect time to acquire the apparatus to initiate the procedure for Macramé.

## Beginner Macramé

Just like anything in life you will Encounter an Endless amount of techniques to start analyzing a new craft or craft. I am not likely to claim for an expert on Macramé. In fact, I'm an entire newbie. From inch new-comer into still another I'll simply take you throughout my private journey to demonstrate one method to execute it.

I shall Provide each of the instruments which you Need to find that your Solution to make the enjoyable art of Macramé. The good thing is you do not have to develop into professional to create definitely amazing decoration bits for you dwelling. Frankly, it seems much tougher as it's. Thus, let us enter it.

First: Exercise precisely the ideal method to do Macramé

Why should the proceedings that you exercise? Like anything that Endeavour is precisely about to price you a tiny bit. Exactly how much? My first 'real' job cost me around $30 because of the Macramé rope (and sometimes even Macramé cord, since it may possibly be understood ) and a few dollars because of its very own wooden dowel.

Macramé Practice job

Reasons why I urge a Little "clinic" job:

It fills time gap as you wait patiently the Macramé rope.

This will give you the Opportunity to get familiar with Different Macramé knots, their own titles and the way to complete them.

By the conclusion of your clinic effort You Are Going to Be Joyful and totally eager to go bigger, or you're getting to see this isn't for you personally.

Completing this clinic effort will Provide you precisely the Assurance to commit your cash and time to choose the subsequent step into to a first "real" Macramé undertaking.

## Next: Exactly What Macramé Job Can I Make?

Make a determination concerning precisely what job you may Need to create. Look over pictures of Macramé on the Web. It's possible to hunt Esty, P-interest, along with Google. Do some researching to master everything exactly is available on the marketplace.

What sorts of Macramé activities will I produce? Start small.

Plant holder

Jewellery such as choker necklaces or bracelets

Wall-hanging

Novel mark

Key string

Bigger jobs comprise:

Dining table

Hammock (rescue a Significant job such as this for later )

Lighting-fixture

Carpet

Headboard

Garland or bunting

Choose the job type. Wall-hangings and plant Holders will most likely be both common new-comer tasks.

Where's it planning to move? This can definitely help determine What dimensions you are attempting to produce.

Locate a design which that suits you . Longer Free form and organic or symmetric with traces which can be fresh and readily defined patterns?

## Where Can I Locate Macramé Patterns?

Whenever you have determined what Sort of job and Design attracts you personally, you are all set to search for a design. I came across my regimen Esty for under 5.

You don't need to get a design. You will find a Gazillion YouTube pictures that could assist you through construction many tasks that you may possibly undoubtedly love. Three Chief reasons I decided to get a blueprint would be:

I had been searching through Esty for suggestions for what Kind of Project I desired to produce and realized at the point that buying patterns was an alternative. I fell in love with work that is been precisely what I'd been imaging.

Patterns are a really inexpensive choice ($5-$10).

I enjoyed the idea of not having to work side by Side working with an image, stopping and starting it frequently. Getting off in my own computer seemed more relaxing for me .

## What Stuff Do Want For Macramé?

Once You have your own project/pattern You're going to Know exactly how much rope to purchase. I presumed that I had to utilize organic cotton collection, however, it's likely to let your personal taste and design show you as you choose your shade & stuff. They promote rope (or cable) around Esty. But, it had been inaccessible at the price or number I desired. Adhering to a great deal of hunting this is the connection which I used.

## What Stuff Do I Need For Macramé?

Whenever you've your project/pattern You're More likely to learn precisely how much rope to purchase. I presumed that I had to utilize organic cotton collection, however, it's likely to let your personal taste and design show you as you choose your shade & stuff. They promote rope (or cable) around Esty. But, it had been inaccessible at the price or number I desired. Adhering to a great deal of hunting this is the connection which I used.

Can I achieve this?

Yes, I am here to let you know can.

Here's a Very Small Behind the scenes confessional of my own experience:

How often could it choose to Learn that a Macramé knot?

Inside my clinic endeavor I lost track of this amount Of times I had to repeat the movie into the beginning and begin. And that I'd have moments after I wondered whether that really was because of me personally. Because of this, it's completely normal to become momentary doubts together side your learning curve.

Selections to the Macramé project if you operate

Under supplies I recorded "rolling clothes Stand" this really is precisely what I used and that was advocated however it's costly and maybe not mandatory for those who never have one.

You Can work together with your dowel or ring Wrapped out of anywhere that's suitable.

You can hang it in a Door Knob, a drawer, or even Anyplace you'll observe to secure your own piece.

Other thoughts would be to use a more suction cup hook or maybe an over-the-door wreath hanger.

You may Defeat a piece of artwork hanging out your walls (temporarily) and hold your bit by the nail.

Assessing outside a diagram, nevertheless well Methodical and clarified that it will likely soon be, won't provide you plenty of assistance to allow you in order to Macramé precisely. It's crucial to find ribbon to have the capability to Macramé effectively. Like some other gained art, attempting to understand just how exactly to Macramé in addition calls for training. Obtain some clear, training samples of diagrams that are simple to secure started. You may quickly realize the ones that are simpler to eventually become more straightforward compared to the intricacies of the ones that are elaborate. You will manage to progress for them with a great deal of exercise and time.

Macramé is your historic craft of knotting rope or fiber Out of distinct patterns to generate decorative and practical services and products. As much early cultures had depicted linking art and techniques styles, the form of Macramé we utilize every single day has its own roots in ancient china. The saying Macramé is in origin, also suggests 'fringe'.

Over time period, Macramé disperse Through the duration of the orient and Europe, thanks partly to both sailors and sea faring merchants, that practiced the art of knot tying for decorative and endurance purposes. Macramé methods were being used from the dark ages to manage mourning jewellery in the own hair, a practice that lasted into the 19th century. From the

Victorian age, Macramé was quite a favourite and stylish pastime in England, used for lace, decorative details, and clothing.

The 1960's and 1970's saw a resurgence of attention in Knotted crafts, together with Macramé plant figurines, wall-hangings, accessories, and jewellery. Vibrant colours and bold designs are part of this minute.

Macramé Turns in a sudden Range of design And dwelling accessory items out available now. From hemp jewellery to woven bag bags, Macramé has generated a primary effect on tendency and also at your home. Now's Macramé features thicker, more calming colours and also a more impressive variety of fibers, textures and antiques. Macramé is actually a fantastic only craft--what you'll need can be just a length of cable, a group of scissors, hooks, along with a function coating, therefore it stores and journeys well.

Besides the basic knot patterns you may Additionally have in order to exercise and focus for just a little before you'll memorize the activities and also create balanced knots. This won't be heard in case you are in a rush, you have to take actions by measure as a way to grasp just how exactly to Macramé. At any time you have mastered the straightforward knot layouts, then move up them to generate simple works such as bracelets. Besides the knots, you then must acquire an eye to coincide with the best colourings to supply the knot out works.

Bracelets are Fantastic for Newbies because the easiest Knots are required without a high volume of elegance. If you feel at ease your skill, then you are able to manage very complex routines. The absolute best confident about complicated and incredibly complex designs is they are sometimes completely shaped to generate decorative items which seem very outstanding.

First, to Choose a time period that would need to grasp the way exactly to Macramé Fully would depend upon several variables like how fast you are able position to comprehend the process. If you are knitting or sewing to receive yourself a protracted period the amount of sophistication needs to be since there really are a few similarities with the practice.

Macramé is a popular way to decorate for decades, Bringing warmth and texture in to a house or apartment with knots that may be placed together in identifying methods of making one of a kind wall hangings, plant holders, and more.

It's Easy to understand the way to Macramé because you Simply should understand a handful knots to get paid a Macramé task.

Obtaining studying to knot

Before you are ready to Begin learning the way to Macramé, Gather your gear and familiarize yourself with a few regular Macramé requirements you will need to grasp.

CHAPTER 1:

# What Is Macramè?

## The Art of Macramé

For men and women who'd like to grasp how-to macramé, there's a range of areas available on the marketplace. Creating complex knots that produce whole patterns that could likewise be transformed to exquisite bracelets, flower baskets and decorative wall-hangings is just what macramé is based on being an art. the exact first and elaborate step in looking to understand just how exactly to macramé, at case that you're interested in this subject, is understanding how the basic knots and a couple of diagrams.

## Beginner Macramé

Just like anything in life you will encounter an endless amount of techniques to start analyzing a new craft or craft. I am not likely to claim for an expert on Macramé. In fact, I'm an entire newbie. From inch newcomer into still another I'll simply take you throughout my private journey to demonstrate one method to execute it.

I shall provide each of the instruments which you need to find that your solution to make the enjoyable art of Macramé. The good thing is you do not have to develop into professional to create definitely amazing decoration bits for you dwelling. Frankly, it seems much tougher as it's. Thus, let us enter it.

First: Exercise exactly the ideal method to do Macramé

Why should the proceedings that you exercise? Like anything that endeavor is exactly about to price you a tiny bit. Exactly how much? My first 'real' job cost me around $30 because of the

Macramé rope (and sometimes even Macramé cord, since it may possibly be understood) and a few dollars because of its very own wooden dowel.

## Macramé Practice Job

Reasons why I urge a little "clinic" job:

It fills time gap as you wait patiently the macramé rope.

This will give you the opportunity to get familiar with different macramé knots, their own titles and the way to complete them.

By the conclusion of your clinic effort you are going to be joyful and totally eager to go bigger, or you're getting to see this isn't for you personally.

Completing this clinic effort will provide you precisely the assurance to commit your cash and time to choose the subsequent step into to a first "real" macramé undertaking.

## Exactly… What Macramé Job Can I Make?

Make a determination concerning exactly what job you may Need to create. Look over pictures of Macramé on the Web. It's possible to hunt Esty, Pinterest, along with Google. Do some researching to master everything exactly is available on the marketplace.

What sorts of Macramé activities will I produce? Start small.

- Plant holder

- Jeweler such as choker necklaces or bracelets

- Wall-hanging

- Novel mark

- Key string

- Bigger jobs comprise:

- Dining table

- Hammock (rescue a significant job such as this)

- Lighting-fixture

- Carpet

- Headboard

- Garland or bunting

Choose the job type. Wall-hangings and plant Holders will most likely be both common new-comer tasks.

Where's it planning to move? This can definitely help determine what dimensions you are attempting to produce.

Locate a design which that suits you. Longer free form and organic or symmetric with traces which can be fresh and readily defined patterns?

## Locating Macramé Patterns

Whenever you have determined what sort of job and design attracts you personally, you are all set to search for a design. I came across my regimen Esty for under 5.

You don't need to get a design. You will find a gazillion YouTube pictures that could assist you through construction many tasks that you may possibly undoubtedly love. Three chief reasons I decided to get a blueprint would be:

I had been searching through Esty for suggestions for what kind of project I desired to produce and realized at the point that buying patterns was an alternative. I fell in love with work that is been precisely what I'd been imaging.

Patterns are a really inexpensive choice ($5-$10).

I enjoyed the idea of not having to work side by Side working with an image, stopping and starting it frequently. Getting off in my own computer seemed more relaxing for me.

## Stuffs That I Need For Macramé

Whenever you've your project/pattern you're more likely to learn precisely how much rope to purchase. I presumed that I had to utilize organic cotton collection, however, it's likely to let your personal taste and design show you as you choose your shade & stuff. They promote rope (or cable) around Esty. But it had been inaccessible at the price or number I desired. Adhering to a great deal of hunting this is the connection which I used.

Can I achieve this?

Yes, I am here to let you know can.

Here's a very small behind the scenes confessional of my own experience:

How often could it choose to Learn that a Macramé knot?

Inside my clinic endeavor I lost track of this amount of times I had to repeat the movie into the beginning and begin. And that I'd have moments after I wondered whether that really was because of me personally. Because of this, it's completely normal to become momentary doubts together side your learning curve.

## Selections To The Macramé Project If You Operate

Under supplies I recorded "rolling clothes stand" this really is exactly what I used and that was advocated however it's costly and maybe not mandatory for those who never have one.

You can work together with your dowel or ring wrapped out of anywhere that's suitable.

You can hang it in a doorknob, a drawer, or even anyplace you'll observe to secure your own piece.

Other thoughts would be to use a more suction cup hook or maybe an over-the-door wreath hanger.

You may Defeat a piece of artwork hanging out your walls (temporarily) and hold your bit by the nail.

Assessing outside a diagram, nevertheless well methodical and clarified that it will likely soon be, won't provide you plenty of assistance to allow you in order to Macramé precisely. It's crucial to find ribbon to have the capability to Macramé effectively. Like some other gained art, attempting to understand just how exactly to Macramé in addition calls for training. Obtain some clear, training samples of diagrams that are simple to secure started. You may quickly realize the ones that are simpler to eventually become simpler compared to the intricacies of the ones that are elaborate. You will manage to progress for them with a great deal of exercise and time.

Macramé is your historic craft of knotting rope or fiber out of distinct patterns to generate decorative and practical services and products. As much early cultures had depicted linking art and techniques styles, the form of Macramé we utilize every single day has its own roots in ancient china. The saying Macramé is in origin, also suggests 'fringe'.

Over time period, Macramé disperse through the duration of the orient and Europe, thanks partly to both sailors and sea faring merchants, that practiced the art of knot tying for decorative and endurance purposes. Macramé methods were being used from the dark ages to manage mourning jeweler in the own hair, a practice that lasted into the 19th century. From the Victorian age, Macramé was quite a favorite and stylish pastime in England, used for lace, lace, lace, decorative details, and clothing.

The 1960's and 1970's saw a resurgence of attention in knotted crafts, together with Macramé plant figurines, wall-hangings, accessories, and jeweler. Vibrant colors and bold designs are part of this minute.

Macramé turns in a sudden range of design and dwelling accessory items out available now. From hemp jeweler to woven bag bags, Macramé has generated a primary effect on tendency and also at your home. Now's Macramé features thicker, more calming colors and also a more impressive variety of fibers, textures and antiques. Macramé is actually a fantastic only craft--what you'll need can be just a length of cable, a group of scissors, hooks, along with a function coating, therefore it stores and journeys well.

Besides the basic knot patterns, you may additionally have in order to exercise and focus for just a little before you'll memorize the activities and also create balanced knots. This won't be heard in case you are in a rush; you have to take actions by measure as a way to grasp just how exactly to Macramé. At any time, you have mastered the very simple knot layouts, then move up them to generate simple works such as bracelets. Besides the knots, you then must acquire an eye to coincide with the best colorings to supply the knot out works.

Bracelets are fantastic for newbies because the easiest knots are required without a high volume of elegance. If you feel at ease your skill, then you are able to manage very complex routines. The absolute best confident about complex and incredibly complex designs is they are sometimes completely shaped to generate decorative items which seem very outstanding.

First, to choose a time period that would need to grasp the way exactly to Macramé fully would depend upon several variables like how fast you are able position to comprehend the process. If you are knitting or sewing to receive yourself a protracted period, the amount of sophistication needs to be since there really are a few similarities with the practice.

Macramé is a popular way to decorate for decades, bringing warmth and texture into a house or apartment with knots that may be placed together in identifying methods of making one-of-a-kind wall hangings, plant holders, and more.

It's easy to understand the way to Macramé because you simply should understand a handful knots to get paid a Macramé task.

## Studying The Knots

Before you are ready to begin learning the way to Macramé, gather your gear and familiarize yourself with a few regular Macramé requirements you will need to grasp.

## Provides And Substances

Here's what you are going to have to know and workout your own Macramé knots:

Macramé cable: that can be any type of cord, twine, or strand made from cotton, jute, or synthetic substance. It arrives in various sizes, colors, and spins. Within this tutorial we found that a 3/16" cotton string provided that rope to acquire clotheslines.

Service: you could require something to link to. Popular choices comprise dowel sticks, branches, hoops, or bands. We used a dowel rod for all these knots.

## Crucial Macramé States

You will find just two or three major Macramé requirements you ought to know before its potential to start.

Working string: either the cable or pair of strings which you utilize to create the real knots.

Filler cable: either the cable or pair of cables your knots wrapping around.

Senet: some knot or collection of knots which can be functioned in replicate.

CHAPTER 2:

# History Of Macramé

To offer people satisfaction in the things they need to use, that's one great design office; to give people pleasure in the things they need to do, that's the other use of it. Although we may now consider the phrasing of this statement old-school, the heart of it still feels important. The theory of decoration by William Morris inspired a whole movement, and it still sounds true today. Think about it: the modern shopper wants to know more and more the story behind the producers and their products. The interest in Etsy shops and makers of small batches continues to increase, with many small brands now boasting cults.

The late 1800s arts and crafts movement focused on the value of crafts made with the hand, more specifically in reaction to rapid industrialization. Although it did not include just one style, it was made up of furniture's, art, wallpaper, textiles, home decoration, and more. Focus: creating high-quality items that computers cannot do the same thing.

A knot is the simple action of connecting two loose ends together. We barely give a second thought to the action, but there's so much more to a knot. Since the earliest humans, Knots have been the constant companion of humanity, using it in practical application and transforming it into mystical, scientific, religious, medical, artistic and decorative objects. Macramé is an example of how people turned the simple act of knotting into an art form.

The fragility of textile objects is a frustrating experience by archaeologists of problems— they disintegrate long before we can uncover them for analysis and documentation. This was the same problem with tracing the macramé's origins. Experts believe that knotting has been with humanity since the need for building and work founded by man.

When so many people think about macramé, they imagine the fruits of the rising popularity of the textile technique in the 1970s— contraptions for hanging plants and glass tabletops, multi-tiered lamp shades, and belts, bags, and other bohemian-favored accessories. While macramé fits in with other patterns from the period— the best way to set a boiling hot fondue pot on top of a macramé doily, obvs— its roots reach back thousands of years across oceans. Many believe that the term "macramé" is derived from the word migramah, or "fringe" which is in Arabic. The first known "macramé's" were Arabic weavers from the 13th century, who began to secure the loose ends of woven textiles, such as towels and shawls by tying decorative knots. Wherever and when macramé received its name, the technique is as old as its basic structure: the knot, which has an almost endless number of variations, countless practical applications, and caused an untold number of headaches when left to its own devices.

Excess folding and filling on sheets and veils are knotted in decorative fringes on the edge of hand loomed fabrics by these craftsmen.

Macramé is mostly favored by women these days, like many fiber crafts, but some of the most famous and popular macromeres were men— sailors, to be more precise. Such sailors also started tying for months at sea and incorporating more practical uses, such as bell pulls and rope ladders. When the ships docked at different ports, the sailors often sold or bartered their jobs, and the macramé art— and the popularization of nautical products such as rope and twine — began to spread to other nations, including China, and what was then known as the "New World."

Sailors made macramé objects at sea in hours when they are not on duty, and when they landed, they sold or bartered them. British and American sailors of the nineteenth century made macramé hammocks, bell fringes, and belts. After most used frequent knots, they called the process "square knotting." Also called "McNamara's Lace" by sailors.

Sailors were not the only evangelists of the macramé. The Moors introduced Spain, which they occupied until the 15th century, to the Arabic knot-tying technique, and eventually, it moved to France and Italy. England Queen Marry II taught her ladies how to macramé in the 17th century; nearly 200 years, during Queen Victoria's reign and the subsequently dubbed Victorian Era, all the fashion was the art form. Macramé details decorated everything from table linen to curtains to bedspreads and was a popular hobby for women of the period. A classic, taught readers how to "work rich trimmings for black and colored costumes, for home wear, garden parties, seaside ramblings, and balls— fairy-like household and underlining decorations..." Many Victorian homes were decorated with this craft.

At the beginning of the feminist movement, Macramé's revival represented a broader cultural dichotomy— on the one hand, many of these women buckled traditional gender norms, such as marriage and motherhood, in search of empowered autonomy and financial and sexual freedoms; on the other, in their spare time, they resurrected a an era known for its They w ere only wild, over- the-top, uninhibited, and grandiose in their approach to the painting. In the 1970s, you would imagine just about everything that was made of macramé.

Sure, the era's greatest macramé pattern was a complete hoot. The macramé owl's history, one of the most omnipresent and absurd examples of the craft, is somewhat enigmatic. Owls have been a popular theme in home decor in the 1970s, and the phenomenon may be related to the United States. The 1971 decision of the Forest Service to appoint Woodsy Owl as their mascot. Following President Richard Nixon's famous trip to China in 1972, Feng Shui became highly marketable in the U.S. and was the mature content for the growing New Age movement.

In 1977, the former Home magazine of the Los Angeles Times not only marketed the macramé owl as THE must-have home decor piece, but also offered a $7.95 DIY kit. When in the early 1980s macramé went out of style again, thousands of once-treasured macramé owls were discarded. The survivors can still be found in thrift shops and on Etsy and look just as dumb as the day they were born.

Macramé all but vanished during the' 80s,' 90s, and' 00s as a home decor trend, but the craft has made a steady return over the past five years. Modern bohemianism includes not only fashion and home decoration, but a whole lifestyle based on personal growth, spiritual development, and the importance of self-care, especially for women. Hobbies with a feminine heritage, including fiber arts such as macramé, have sparked interest; thanks to Facebook, eBay, Pinterest, and other social and e-commerce sites, modern macramé has sparked interest.

We tried to hide things from the 70's very far away, as with many items from the 70's, and macramé vanished again. Popular artist medium. There have been dedicated artists since the 1970s who have brought macramé from a household craft to galleries of artists all over the world. And this is no different from our present day. There are people who pay attention to the return of the macramé with the return of the houseplant phenomenon. This can also explain why ball plants have become a hit in Japanese art. But these are more expensive and difficult to manufacture and not suitable for all plants, so a plant hanger is a good alternative.

Macramé art was based on a number of practical artefacts. At the same time, artists in Portugal, Ecuador and Mexico continued to develop chalks and purses as indigenous craft, while Macramé now focuses on several objects.

I have found a very interesting special macramé application that relates to the practical application of knot tying in life. While I was researching, I came across a blog describing a paracord bracelet that is popular with survivors and outdoors, and it's a macramé bracelet.

And as one of my favorite video bloggers on the internet always say that fashion isn't an island, it's a response. We now know that macramé took shape as a gateway to the world of mass production during the 60s and 70s as part of the massive revival in crafts. One idea that sounds real is with the consciousness of the millennial generation of living a greener lifestyle and a desire to live closer to nature, but this is difficult for many in small apartments without a garden. So, it's the best thing to hang gardens. This may also be the reason why kokedamas Japanese art has become such a phenomenon.

Another interesting part is how macramé and other craft skills are used by different countries and their people as income in impoverished areas. Research suggests that macramé art has now been adopted in Ghana as one of the most important fashion accessory manufacturing methods. This art form is now an alternative method, particularly for the production of bags and shoes in the fashion industry. Over the past few years, the number of younger consumers of macramé products has increased. Today's youth are trendy and focus on new creative designs. Today macramé art is not just a youth work, but a recognition of the creative development of Ghanaian youth's creativity.

Today, Macramé's talent and hobby means many things to many people; in many respects, the talent is valuable and unique, although it doesn't matter to some. Macramé includes bonds that will secure the arms and hands. It can be very relaxing and therapeutic for the body, mind and spirit to make a macramé product; it is also a choice for environmentally friendly art. These are just others of the benefits that macramé art lovers believe their practitioners derive from this art form.

**CHAPTER 3:**

# The Basics Of Macramé (Terminologies)

While macramé has become quite a popular art, in some patterns there are still many words and abbreviations that people may not be aware of or may not know the meaning of.

Adjacent: next to each other.

Alternating– Attach a knot to one cord and then move to tie another cord to the same knot.

ASK– Alternating knots of the square. This abbreviation is often used in macramé patterns because square knots are commonly used.

Band– A long and smooth piece of macramé.

Bar– A set of knots in the design that create an elevated position.

Bight– A small folded cord portion that is forced through the knot's other sections.

Body– You're working on the main section of the project.

Braid– Braids are sometimes also known as plaits and are formed to loop around each other by connecting three or four cords.

Braided cord– A type of cord consisting of several thinner pieces of cord woven together. Twisted cords tend to be more durable than twisted cords.

Bundles– A series of cords that have been stored.

Knot button– A tight, round decorative knot.

BH– The button's door. Vertical lark head nodes are used to create a loop that could be used for fastening or joining parts.

Chinese Macramé– Knotted designs from China and other countries in Asia.

Combination knot– To create a new type of knot or design feature, use two or more knots.

Cords– Cords is any fiber material that is used to build projects with macramé.

Core– The cord / s running through a project's center and knotting around it. These are sometimes referred to as fillers or main strings.

Crook– The curved part of a cord loop.

Diagonal– A line or row of knots extending from top right to bottom (or vice versa) Diagonal knots such as half-hitch knots are often used in macramé designs.

Diameter– The width usually in millimeters of a cord.

DDH – Half hitch double. This concept of macramé means connecting two knots of half-hitch next to each other.

Fillers– cords that remain at the core of a pattern and are knotted around it. Also referred to as core cords.

Findings– objects and fastenings other than cords that can be used to construct loops, fasteners and other functional objects or decorations in macramé designs. There are examples of ear wires and clasps.

Finishing knot– A knot tied to secure the ends of the cord and to prevent them from unravelling.

Fringe– Cord ends lengths not knotted but left suspended.

Knots of fusion– Another term for knots of combination.

Gusset– A term used to design a 3D project's sides like a bag.

Hitch– A knot commonly used to tie cords to other items.

Interlace– Cords are intertwined and woven together to link various areas.

Cord knotting– the cord used in a design to tie the knots.

LH– Knot of the head of larks.

Loop– The circular or oval shape created by the crossing of two parts of a cord.

Micro-Macramé– Macramé projects made using materials that are delicate or small in diameter. Micro-macramé is often defined as any macramé using cords with a diameter of less than 2 mm.

Mount– An object that is used as part of a macramé project, such as a brace, frame or handle. For example: cords mounted on wooden handles at the beginning of a project with a macramé bag.

Natural– Generally this term is used to refer to cords and refers to any material made from plants, wood and other natural substances such as hemp and cotton.

Netting– A series of knots with open spaces between them. Netting is often used to build things like bags and hangers for plants.

OH– Knot overhand.

Picot– Loops on the sides of a design that stand out. These are seen more often in early trends.

Plait– Cords are plated in an alternating pattern by crossing three or more. Also referred to as a braid.

Scallops– Knots loops created along the edges of the design of a macramé.

Segment– Common knot, cord or design areas.

Seniti– This term, also known as a sonnet, is a single chain of identical knots.

Standing end– The cord end was secured on a macramé board or other surface and did not build knots.

SK– Square knot– A common knot created by attaching two cords to one or more cords.

Stitch– Stitch is sometimes used instead of knot in early patterns.

Synthetic – Man-made fibers such as polypropylene and nylon.

Vertical– from top to bottom to top.

Vintage– A pattern, knot, or technique popular in or earlier in the early 1900s. Some vintage knots and patterns are still being used unchanged in macramé today, although others have evolved or disappeared.

Weaving– Weaving cords means placing them under each other or over each other.

Working cord– Another term used to knot cord. The cord with which you are currently working.

CHAPTER 4:

# Decoration And Practical Use

## Garden (Modern and Classic)

### Pet leash

It is quite easy to work out or create the pet leash, and beginners can easily get their way around it. Your animals or pets will definitely love it. This design is very flexible and easy to make as well as use depending on your taste; the knots to be used for the strap depends on what you want as a part of the flexibility of this design. This design can look like the pet collar if the same type of decorative knots are used, but it is NOT the same as the pet collar design

Tools to be used:

• Swivel Hook • Glue • 4mm or 6mm cord material • Project board and pins • The knots to be used are: • Square Knots (SK) • Overhand Knot • Buttonhole Clasp • Vertical Larks Head Knot (Vertical LHK)

Calculations:

• The length of the material (Leash) after the work is done should be determined by you and after you and after it has been selected, you should try out this calculation • Length of leash(Ll in inches) = WC (Wc)/3 (in yards) • The length of the Holding cord also increases by 0.5 yards for every 10 inches the length of leash is beginning from 20 inches which is 2 yards long (i.e., 20 inches = 2 yards, 30 inches = 2.5 yards, 40 inches = 3 yards…..) till you get to your desired leach's length.

• The total amount of materials needed is, therefore dependent on this calculation.

Steps

Put the two cords vertically on our board after getting their corresponding midpoints and tightly place them close to one another. The longer WC should be on the left because that is what will be used to tie the LHK on the HC

A half of the vertical LHK should be made to move using the Wc over or under (as the case may be) the Hc so as to have a counterclockwise loop. Gradually pulling it left, you should make it go over the WC so as to get the crossing point. Once the crossing point is gotten, tie the other half of the Vertical LHK by passing the Wc under or over the Hc, while pulling it left, pass it under the WC to also make the crossing point.

More Vertical LHK should be tied and should be done from the center in the direction of one end. When the first half of the handle is 6 inches, you should stop.

The whole sennit or cords should be rotated and back to the center, leaving the WC on the right. Loos should be made in clockwise directions as tying of Knots is resumed, and once the handle attains a length of 12 inches, you should stop

The four segments should be brought together, thereby folding the sennit. Locate the WC in the process. Tie a SK using the 2 Wc, and it should be tight. The fillers are going to be the short cords

Folding the 2 WC means we should have 4 cords to work with. A suitable decorative knot by the user should be used alongside this wonderful design, some of the best knots to use alongside it are; the Square Knot, the Vertical larks head and the Half hitches with holding cords. A minimum of six inches material should be attached to the hook at the end of the pet leach.

To attach the hook, two cords should be passed through the loop that is on the hook, and a tight finishing should be tied with the four cords. The usage of glue comes in here as the four cords are being tightened, the glue should be used. When it gets dry, all additional materials should be removed or cut to make the work very neat and beautiful. You may also consider another finishing style which entails that you move the ends in the direction of the strap and put it under the back of the knots so that it can be very firm.

## Home Décor

### Macramé Charm and Feather Décor

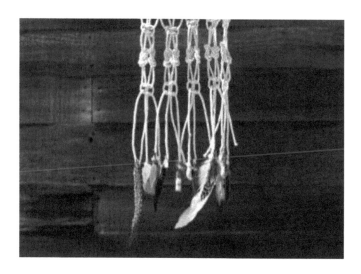

Charms and feathers always look cool. They just add a lot of that enchanting feeling to your house and knowing that you could make Macramé décor with charms and feathers really take your crafting game to new heights! Check out the instructions below and try it out for yourself!

What you need:

- Stick/dowel

- feathers and charms with holes (for you to insert the thread in)

- Embroidery/laundry rope (or any other rope or thread that you want)

Instructions:

Cut as many pieces of rope as you want. Around 10 to 12 pieces is good, and then fold each in half. Make sure to create a loop at each end, like the ones you see below:

Then, go and loop each piece of thread on the stick.

Make use of the square knot and make sure you have four strands for each knot. Let the leftmost strand cross the two strands and then put it over the strands that you have in the middle. Tuck it under the middle two, as well.

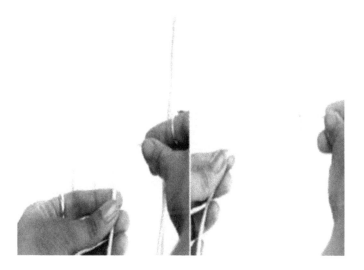

Check under the strands and let the rightmost strand be tucked under the loop to the left-hand strand.

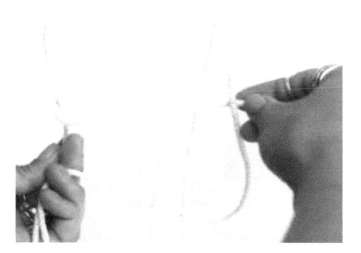

Tighten the loop by pulling the outer strands together and start with the left to repeat the process on the four strands. You will then see that a square knot has formed after tightening the loops together.

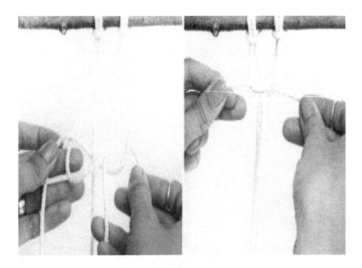

Connect the strands together by doing square knots with the remaining four pieces of rope and then repeat the process again from the left side. Tighten the loop by pulling the outer strands together and start with the left to repeat the process on the four strands. You will then see that a square knot has formed after loops have been tightened together.

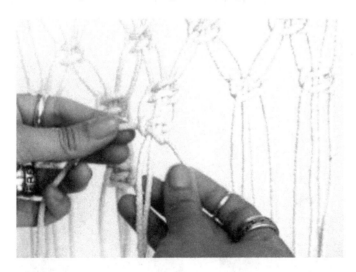

You can then do a figure eight knot and then just attach charms and feathers to the end. Glue them in and burn the ends for better effect!

## Macramé Wall Art

Adding a bit of Macramé to your walls is always fun because it livens up the space without making it cramped—or too overwhelming for your taste. It also looks beautiful without being too complicated to make. You can check it out below!

What you need:

- Large wooden beads

- Acrylic paint

- Painter's tape

- Scissors

- Paintbrush

- Wooden dowel

- 70 yards rope

Instructions:

Attach the dowel to a wall. It's best just to use removable hooks so you won't have to drill anymore.

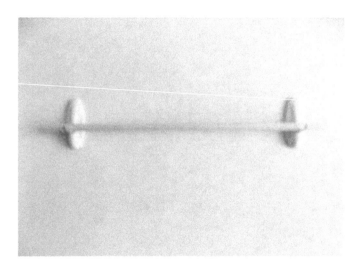

Cut the rope into 14 x 4 pieces, as well as 2 x 5 pieces. Use 5-yard pieces to bookend the dowel with. Continue doing this with the rest of the rope.

Then, start making double half-hitch knots and continue all the way through, like what's shown below.

Once you get to the end of the dowel, tie the knots diagonally so that they wouldn't fall down or unravel in any way. You can also add the wooden beads any way you want, so you'd get the kind of décor that you need. Make sure to tie the knots after doing so.

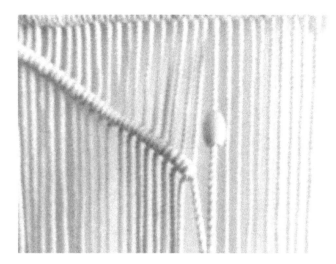

Use four ropes to make switch knots and keep the décor all the more secure. Tie around 8 of these.

Add a double half hitch and then tie them diagonally once again.

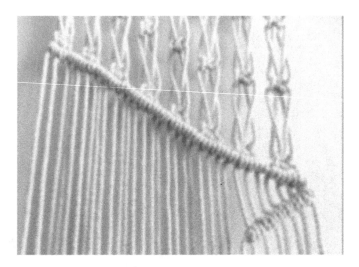

Add more beads and then trim the ends of the rope.

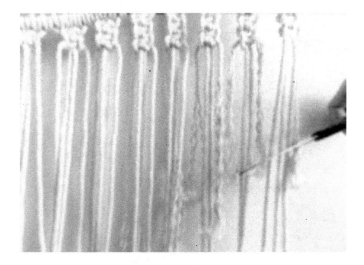

Once you have trimmed the rope, go ahead and add some paint to it. Summery or neon colors would be good.

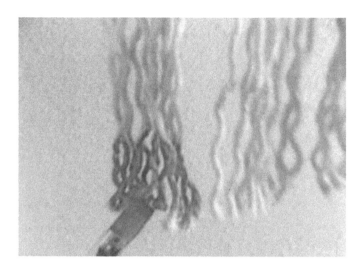

That's it! You now have your own Macramé Wall Art!

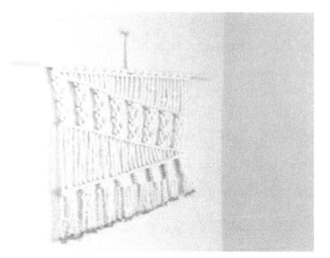

CHAPTER 5:

# Health Benefits Of Macramé Hangers

The craft was so popular in the seventies that practically everybody's decks would be embellished with macramé wall mounts of numerous colors and utilizing various kinds of macramé cables. More plant wall mounts might be discovered to bring indoor plants in the living room and the cooking area, where large windows would open to the yard, letting the breeze in.

The macramé plant wall mounts made terrific concepts for a craft task or for a handcrafted present for a good friend. The craft is so simple to do. It can be carried out simply one day and even half a day. Kids were taught to macramé by their grannies, aunties, and mommies.

Having indoor plants gets rid of approximately 96% of carbon monoxide gas from a space every day, according to research studies performed by NASA. Particular plants are understood to get rid of other bad contaminants, such as formaldehyde, from the air. This nasty toxic substance can be discovered in all sorts of unwary locations, such as a brand-new carpet, or artificial upholstery.

To begin with, plants produce needed oxygen; soak up toxic substances and co2; tidy up the VOCs released by plastics, carpet fibers, paint, and artificial structure products that trigger Sick Building Syndrome, headaches, aching, dry throats, scratchy or dry skin, and tiredness; assist individuals in recuperating rapidly from an illness, and develop a calmer and more calming environment. Making macramé plant wall mounts, or offering one as a present, motivates growing indoor plants. What more thoughtful present could you provide to liked ones in your house than developing a healthy environment? And what much better method to present indoor plants into the house than with some upgraded, modern-day macramé wall mounts?

Keep in mind, making macramé plant wall mounts for your house or as presents, and it is not an easy plant wall mount. Keeping that in mind, it's time to get your macramé cables and begin knotting!

The Flower Power generation had it right the very first time. There is a health advantage in surrounding your household with flowers and green plants. An excellent way to grow plants and flowers is to plant them in pots and to hang some utilizing macramé plant wall mounts.

Exactly what can macramé plant wall mounts provide for your health? As it ends up, indoor Plants Offer Lots Of Health Advantages, Aside From Being Popular House Designs.

## Beautiful Craft Of Macramé Plant Hanger

This wall mount is a fantastic present which can be provided out to your liked ones. With macramé plant wall mounts, you have the option of either keeping your plants inside your home or outdoors without any damage to the plants. Macramé plant wall mount is amongst the different types of macramé, which is restoring the attention it should have. Plant wall mounts are one of the most popular products in the gorgeous art of macramé.. Macramé plant wall mount is suitable for revealing off your plants. You can put your potted plants in the wall mount to provide an incredible and natural appearance.

The different colors of the macramé plant wall mount offer you the chance to choose the ones that fit your taste. If utilized as outside plant wall mounts, guarantee your color option matches the basic tone of the structure. The craft of macramé plant wall mount is taken by some individuals as a pastime. You have fewer products to utilize for this reason minimizes intricacies associated with some crafts.

Macramé plant wall mount is ending up being the style now. Macramé plant wall mount is a craft that is natural. In conclusion, the lovely craft -macramé plant wall mount has actually come to remain. Let's utilize it to show our plants for a more natural touch in the house, work environment, gallery, and so on

**CHAPTER 6:**

# The Essential Tools And Materials You Need To Have

The utilitarian origins of Macramé's were with jute, hemp, and linen, as well as other fibers, which were mainly used for nets and cloth. As sailors and merchants collected different types of material from the lands to which they sailed, they helped to build the craft — and also to pass it on.

Fast-forward to modern-day, where we have new technology, fabrics, and, of course, the Internet, and you have the most amazing collection of fibers and beads and discoveries to produce just about anything you can imagine.

However, Macramé requires more than just fiber, beads, and findings. Many of the tools that you'll need to build the projects you probably already own in this book. You can quickly buy something you don't have on hand at your local bead or craft store or, in some cases, even your local hardware store.

## Macramé Boards

Macramé projects need to be fixed to a surface while you work-usually with T pins and/or masking tape. This makes it easier to deal with your cords and helps to keep the knots secure and neatly aligned. In your local bead or craft shop, or via online retailers, specially made macramé boards are available and work for most projects. They are usually around 12" / 18" (30 cm / 46 cm) and made of fiberboard. Most macramé boards created have a grid on the surface and rulers along the sides. They can be removed, but I leave them in place shrink-wrapped or sealed, as I consider them very helpful guides when I am working. Some also include the simple macramé knots as instructional illustrations.

If your project is too large to fit on a regular macramé board, you may need to create your own. Choose a porous surface; you can pin your work easier too. You'll also want to select a surface that you can easily and without damage adhere to, remove, and reposition tape repeatedly. I have used the surface of an old desk for broader ventures. For a long curtain, I once designed a wooden board of 3' some 6' (91 cm some 183 cm) to get the job done. If you end up making your own macramé surface, then you're going to want to draw a grid on it and add rulers to the sides. If you are working on an unorthodox surface, such as a table or airplane tray, you might also want to attach a piece of tape with measurements written on it, so that you have a guide close to you.

## Pins And Tape Pins

Using pins, your project is secured to your macramé board, so it doesn't move around as you work. They also come in handy when you integrate different knot sequences and other design elements into your projects to keep those strands in place.

The most common option for macramé is t-pins. They have a good length, and their form makes it easy for them to insert and remove again and again. This is also possible to use ball-end pins used for sewing, but they are not quite as robust as T-pins. Stop replacing push pins and thumbtacks, which are both too short.

It also uses masking tape to bind materials to the work surface. If you're working on a more fragile surface, it can be a replacement for T-pins, but it's most widely used to secure "filler cords" — or cords that you tie your working cords around — while tying square and twisting knots. (On the following pages, you'll read more about these.) I prefer the blue painter's masking tape because it appears to be easier to remove and reposition while you work than standard masking press. Avoid removing duct tape, packaging tape, or any other transparent tape; they're all too sticky and can damage your cords and surface, and are hard to remove all over.

## Scissors

Many macramé projects are made from thin fibers, which are easy to cut with a simple pair of design scissors like those you probably already own. You may want to get a pair of little trimming scissors made for sewing to trim the excess length when a project is complete. They'll let you really get close to any knot you want to cut.

Any of the projects mentioned in this book use hide and cord suede and leather. Those need to cut a more powerful pair of scissors. From the leather store, there are wonderful economic scissors which have been my favorite great all-around scissors. They can handle the hides, but they are small enough to cut ends around knots, and they're perfect for just about all the rest. If you're planning to work with these materials frequently, getting a higher-quality pair of scissors is worth the investment.

## Adhesives

Most macramé designs are done by using adhesive to protect the final knot(s). The type of adhesive that should be used will depend on the materials used. Waxed linen, hemp, cotton, silk, and other fibers are perfect for white glue. Leather and suede are ideally suited for rubber cement or contact cement. E-6000 and epoxy are very strong adhesives used to glue non-porous objects together, such as wire and even labradorite beads, which are used for the buckle of the heart belt. Both of these adhesives require adequate ventilation during use and should be enforced strictly by all warning labels. My personal favorite is The Third! , Very solid and versatile, nontoxic, water-based super glue. Bear in mind the toxicity of the glue when deciding which adhesive is best to use for your project, particularly if it will come into contact with the skin.

## Cords

If you can tie in a knot, you'll probably be able to macramé with it. Waxed-linen and waxed hemp are two of the most common fiber styles for working with. They come in a wide range of colors and thicknesses. The wax coating on those cords helps them incredibly well keep a knot. Your knots and knot patterns that result will be well described. Those cords are sold by bead and craft shops, or you can easily find them online.

Another popular macramé material is rattail, a satin cord that comes in a colored rainbow and at least three distinct thicknesses. In the 1970s, Rattail was popular but never gone out of style with artisans who like to integrate Chinese Knots or Celtic Knots into their work. It can be slippery, and if not fixed, well knots tied in rattail will loosen. But the results look so beautiful it really is worth using this stuff.

My lifelong favorite is polypropylene or polyolefin chain. It is used to make rope for boating, traveling, and any vocation that needs a very sturdy, robust, waterproof material. It's perfect for purses, hammocks, or even the leash and collar project as well. The array of colors is not that big, but the practical properties make it a reasonable choice for certain ventures. This can be found at your nearest hardware store.

Leather and lace suede are fantastic fabrics made from macramé. There are a number of lace weights available. Look for the softer and more supple laces, and avoid stiffer ones that may be hard to tie. Consider the shape and purpose of your project when determining which type of hiding you want to use. Is it a jackpot? An asshole? Does the material have to be tough and ready to smash, or will it be handled more sensitively? There's a small, soft suede I've used for tiny bags, a beaded curtain, and even a necklace, but I know from experience that a bigger bag will need a thicker and more durable lace. Ultra- Suede is an alternative to leather and suede. Ultra-suede is a synthetic fabric that resists stains and has a very similar feeling to suede but is machine washable. It comes in a wide range of colors and a few different thicknesses. Countless leather, suede, and ultra-suede sizes, designs, and colors are available in your local bead, art, or leather shop, as well as online.

In some of the accessories in this book, cotton and wool yarns are used like a scarf, a belt, and even a halter top. There are so many beautiful yarns out there, and I must confess that I have always been a little jealous of knitters and all their choices! But I have no desire to knit. I do want the yarn, though. Experiment with your options as you are going to the yarn store. You can find varying textures in bamboo yarn, cashmere, alpaca, angora, and more in addition to can cotton and wool blends. My favorites are the chunky, variegated yarns (like the one I used for the scarf). Treat yourself to luscious, hand-tinted fibers.

The key things to consider when determining which sort of yarn to use: How well does it knot? If the material is too slippery, then the knot may fall out. Have you got enough material? In the case of certain specialty yarns, all they can get can be what they have in stock. With a backpack on which I was working, I found this the hard way. I just bought two yarn skeins, though they had three. I used one skein per handle when I installed the yarn to the handles and noticed that I didn't have enough yarn to complete the project. The last skein had, of course, been sold out. Oops. Oops. I managed to get nice, neutral cotton that matched to fill in, but that day I sure learned a lesson. Often it is easier to buy all the particular colors to make sure you have enough products. It's easier to have extra than not necessary.

## Wire

The wire is a hard material to use for macramé — but if you master the craft, the results can be unique pieces of jewelry. The essence of metal is not to bend over and over again. It lacks strength, and repetitive bending causes the wire to become brittle and work-hardened. If you bend it back and forth, again and again, it will finally crack. Heavier wire also doesn't like to bend without a huge amount of effort. Most metal macramé is made from thinner gauge wire, which is easier to manipulate. When it's working, it will always stiffen, but the less you bend it, the better.

If you haven't dealt with wire before, you might want to get more acquainted with it first by using a less costly metal wire. There are several wire types to choose from, including brass, copper, and art wire, which come in a bunch of different colors. Most of these tubes, also known as gauges, are available in different thicknesses. Because of its thickness, the lower the gauge number is, the thicker the wire is hard to bend.

# CHAPTER 7:

# Detailed & Illustrated Patterns And Projects You Can Start With

I enjoy dangling plants at my porch at the time of summer and spring months. It also gives it a very pretty look, and it's a perfect way to hold an eye on my more responsive plants. I have a nice little surprise for you if you enjoy dangling plants; however, I really don't want to waste the money on the plant hanger bought in store. I find twenty DIY dangling plantings, which are all very cheap and simple to create. You may hang them in the interior of your house or put these to the deck to put elegance and color to any space.

Plant hangers aren't hard to produce at all, and the stuff you can repurpose and revamp to create them really don't believe you. You can find the ideal dangling plant from antique cages of birds to empty coconuts to give the house the desired look you like. Dangling plants in the house not only put the appeal, but keeping those rising plants inside is very safe for everyone in the house. And, all of these are so simple that you may prefer to make all of them. They are guaranteed to make you improve your house lawn.

You don't even have to pay a lot or run yourself in desperation to have a wonderful garden and house. With simply a few bucks and some hours, you can make the very beautiful DIY dangling planters that will present such color and style to the porch and house! If you simply want to make your garden and house better this summer and spring, you simply need to try out some dangling planters.

## 1. Easy Dangling Planter

In case you require something that is super simple and cheap, it's this dangling planter. You can do it with a cheap Walmart, Dollar, or Target Store planter and then only attach your dangling rope to it. Putting this one together takes only a couple minutes, and in case you decided to modify it a little more, you might paint whatever color you choose to suit your current decor to the planters.

## 2.  The Planter Of Revamped Bird Cage

These cool antique cages can be sold in thrift shops, and these are very cheap. Do not worry if these cages have dents, even if they are little damaged even missing, that only put the charm of the rustic. Simply furnish it with the desired plants until you've got the cage and cover it with twine, rope or string. It is a smart place to get a gorgeous planter suitable for dangling indoors or outdoors.

### 3. Planter of Revamped Coconut

As I prefer fresh coconut; however, I don't know how to use shells except maybe chuck them away. That is a very safer concept here. Transform the shell of hollow coconut into a grower! You should simply create a coconut in two planters. These are great for succulents planting, or you may put a tiny floral house to them. When you're searching for a nice presence on the shore, coconuts may be the best dangling planters.

### 4. Planter of Dangling Beaded

Only the ten-dollar cost of supplies offers you everything you require to build a lovely dangling planter. To build this one, you need only a jar, twine or rope, and some fancy beads. It's super simple and simply takes a little amount of time to complete. These create great presents in case you know someone who enjoys dangling plants and adding some lovely greenery, they maybe hang them on the porch, indoors, or roof.

### 5. Upgrading of DIY Dangling Planter

With only a few materials and a little amount of time, take every ordinary dangling planter and transform it into something amazing. This is very gorgeous and simple to do. To make it beautiful you want a simple vine, and then a little paint with other decoration. You may do any style or paint scheme you require to suit your other decor.

### 6. DIY Dangling Wall Planters of Wooden

Well, you don't have to actually have twine or string to admire the lovely dangling planters. These walls of wooden planting devices are very simple to create and cheap, and also, they stick straight on the walls. Moreover, these are perfect for succulents planting, or you might give them a bigger one and bring in the larger plants. Hang them in the building, or on a porch or roof. To spread out your yard, hang it closer to the succulent DIY garden.

## 7. DIY Dish Planter Dangling of Pleated

This gorgeous patterned Umbra dish is ideal for building a DIY planter dangling. You may utilize whatever dish you have well. A simple jar will fit for that one. Only build the dangler from twine rope and Bind it to your house's ceiling or on the covered roof or porch.

## 8. Beautiful DIY Water Garden Dangling

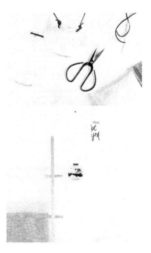

A dangling planter does not actually carry any other plants in the building. You can build a beautiful dangling water garden that can provide you the greenery you desire and put a truly unique feel to space. For this reason, a revamped fish tank is ideal, and you may install any water plant you desire. Stones and other decorations give it a very good look, and you can bring this one together in simply five minutes.

### 9. DIY Bindred Planter Dangling

A few planters of wire in some paint and various widths are simply about what you want to make this beautiful DIY dangling Bindred plantings. In case you have some wired baskets, you may add as many thirds as you like. To offer them a completely special appearance, you may paint them in various kinds of colors and put beads and other decorations. This is very simple and good for getting different plants that you desire to put.

### 10. DIY Pansy Ball Dangling

A dangling floral ball can be a lovely way to bring much color to every space in your house. This is created from pansies and put together is super simple. You don't see planter anyway. You simply see a pretty flower ball that you may hang from either outdoors or indoors. You create it from two inexpensive dangling basketball planters, then bring them close to create a ball shape.

### 11. Reused Embroidery Hoop Planter Dangling

I adore this reused planter with the embroidery. You may create these with the size of the embroidery hoop you have at present, considering your plant or dish suits inside it. It can be a very beautiful dangling planter and makes it very simple. In case you have any old dishes to reuse, you may utilize them and render it a fully repurposed planting project.

### 12. DIY Dangling of Wooden Shelf

This dangling planter is constructed from a plate of wood and has a gorgeous rustic feel to it. In case you don't have a plate which you may utilize, well, if you got the proper equipment, you can easily make one yourself. Then you only have to pick something to attach with – string, twine, and so on – then put planter to the disc made of wood.

### 13. Revamped Tire Dangling Planter

The old tire you found in the lawn will make a great planter. Well, there're many styles you may revamp used tires, and my favorites are this one. You're simply dangling the tire from a tree and attaching the plant to it – yeah, there's a little more effort involved than that, but it's a really simple and imaginative idea.

### 14. DIY Jar (Mason) Planter Dangling

I love projects with a mason jar, really. Each one is too simple to build and so beautiful when it's finished. You can need a vacant jar to build a plant and then cover it with cords, or if you like the rustic feel of the farmhouse, you might use twine. For small plants, this is a perfect project as well as you may hang these jars indoors or outdoors.

## 15. DIY Ball Planter of Moss Dangling

These ball planters can be very good and simple to make. In reality, it is the best and least costly DIY dangling planters you might make. To build it, you need simply dirt, some cords, and moss, obviously your chosen vine. With these or also tiny flowering plants, you might do succulents so you will render your moose balls as tiny or as big as you want them.

## 16. Reused Inverted Planters Dangling

Well, I do love those dangling inverted planters. They're so amusing and look amazing on the deck or inside your house. These are really simple to produce, and you use recycled products to build them, so they're pretty cheap too. It can be a perfect idea to repurpose some hollow coffee containers, or if you like them to be a little bigger, you might utilize tin cans or 2 Liter bottles.

## 17. Revamped Plastic Bottle Planters Dangling

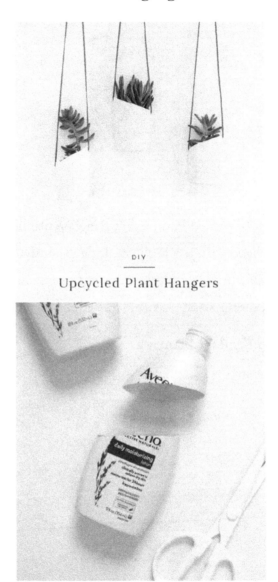

We all know these used bottles of shampoo, conditioner, and lotion you put out whenever they are vacant? Can we turn these in a beautiful dangling planter? As these are really simple, and they are also super cheap to make as you're utilizing vacant bottles. To make them attractive, you'll need to cut these bottles a little and cover or paint them up. However, it can be a very simple project, and also these might happen to be some great gifts.

### 18. Dangling of Wooden Basket Planter

A few lightweight baskets can be turned into elegant dangling planters. And, you can only check out those gorgeous ones I find on Etsy. They're really inexpensive, around 10 dollars each of them, and you only put the plants on the deck once you get them. You may also use such in house, and they also have a beautiful rustic look, which is ideal for decorating your farmhouse.

### 19. Dangling of Wooden Pendant Planter

To decorate any room in your house, create these gorgeous pendant dangling planters. These are very easy to produce and look so lovely and special to them. And you may utilize them to grow smaller plants such as some small plants which don't require much space. I can be an ideal approach to put some color to the house, and you're literally not going to admit how much easy it is to produce.

CHAPTER 8:

# Step-By-Step Instructions And Professional Advice For Macramè Home And Garden Décor

## DIY Tassel and Macramé Keychains

W ho doesn't love a sweet ring? Particularly a lovely DIY version which takes no time to make, uses stuff you've already got, can be as simple or as fantastic as you want? If you need an excuse to make a personalized keychain, we have you:

Update your keychain before remembering it, create a replacement set of keys for your domestic pet sitter, make a replacement set of keys you can leave from your neighbor so that when you lockout you have not to break into your own place.

Materials needed for Macramé Keychains

•Key Ring

•3/16" Natural Cotton Piping Cord

•Beads

•Embroidery yarn or floss

•Scissors

You can make things fancy on your keychains tassel or macramé by wrapping them in different yarn or floss colors.

## DIY Round Macramé Boho Coasters

I don't seem to be able to rest every time I find a craft idea, until I know how to do that, these coasters are the perfect example, I've done a macramé bracelet before, but to make a macramé round is strange for me. After exploring the internet, finding some confusing posts, and making my first coaster after ways to create it. That's the way I found it easier (although there's another one I tested as well) and it also got me the most beautiful result.

Supplies:

•3 mm cotton cord

•Something to hold the cords, a cork coaster or a board, either tape or as I used it.

•Pins to hold if the cork is used.

•Fabric Scissors

•Ruler or measuring tape

•Comb

## Boho Christmas Trees

Cut the yarn in 7-8-inch bits. Take two strands and fold them in half in order to form a loop. Place one of the loops under a twig. Start with the bowed end of the other strand and move the ends of the strand under the twig through the loop. Thread through the loop below the twig the ends of that strand. Pull tightly and repeat, okay? If you have added enough knotted strands, use a brush or a comb to separate the threads. The "almost finished" tree is going to be a little floppy so you have to stiffen it with some starch.

When erect, cut the Boho Christmas trees into a triangle shape and decorate them with small baubles or beads. I just made the jewelry wire a little flower star. They're going to take about 10 minutes to make a whole bunch. I think they'd make beautiful gifts, or you could hang them on your Christmas tree.

## Friendship Bracelet Watch

You'll need your watch face and floss to get started. I use art floss in the colors of brown, white and minty blue. Cut strips approximately 48 inches long. You will need 10 of these long strands for each side for this watch face (but just cut 10 right now, leave the others until you're ready to start from the other side). To start making our harness, we will lash each piece of floss onto the chain. Bring together the ends of a long piece of floss and pick up the end. Push through the bar and pull the ends through the loop you've built. Start with all your floss cutting. Make sure you keep the colors in your pattern as you want them. I wanted thick orange and mint stripes and thin white stripes. My order was, therefore: orange, orange, white, mint, mint, mint, mint, mint, white, orange, orange.

And now you're just starting to braid your friendship. We won't have this weird thing bundled up in most friendship bracelets that begins with a knot, because we've latched on the message. Pretty better, huh? You have the choice, like any other friendship bracelet, to twist and then tie when you are wearing it. This is not the most beautiful option, but it's going to work well. But if you want to use closures, continue reading.

You want to take a decent amount of glue when you get the length and run a line where you need to cut. Apply the glue on the front and back sides of the threads. This will hold the braid securely together. I used the fast-dry tacky glue from Aleena because I'm very impatient. I didn't think about this and I had to shorten my straps after a few wears. Perhaps you'd like to go ahead and make the watch a bit tight. The first wear may be uncomfortable, but it will be perfect for a couple of hours. Use sharp scissors to cut the area where you applied the glue through your strap. See how well it sticks with each other? Go ahead and run a little at the very end to help avoid fraying. Place the clamp on the end of the straps and use the pin to lock on firmly. Finish with a jumping ring on one and a jumping ring and closing on the other.

And you got it there! It's a pretty fun wear watch and brings in a new way the whole trend of the friendship bracelet. What do you think about it? Are you going to make one? It sounds like a great project for me on the weekend!

Rainbows might appear childish to your teenagers, yet this rainbow wall dangling from Lia Griffith is tasteful enough to be equally whimsical and mature. This DIY project would appear charming in a childhood bedroom or living area and may be customized with distinctive colors. Take a look at the tutorial to get extra info.

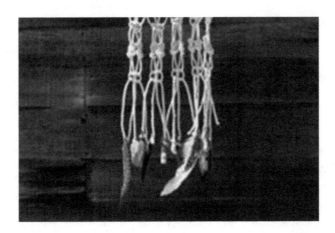

## Macramé Charm and Feather Décor

Charms and feathers always look cool. They just add a lot of that enchanting feeling to your house and knowing that you could make Macramé décor with charms and feathers really take your crafting game to new heights! Check out the instructions below and try it out for yourself!

What you need:

Stick/dowel

feathers and charms with holes (for you to insert the thread in)

Embroidery/laundry rope (or any other rope or thread that you want)

Instructions:

Cut as many pieces of rope as you want. Around 10 to 12 pieces is good, and then fold each in half.

Make sure to create a loop at each end, like the ones you see below:

Then, go and loop each piece of thread on the stick.

Make use of the square knot and make sure you have four strands for each knot. Let the leftmost strand cross the two strands and then put it over the strands that you have in the middle. Tuck it under the middle two, as well.

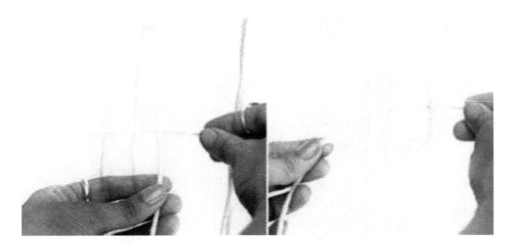

Check under the strands and let the rightmost strand be tucked under the loop to the left-hand strand.

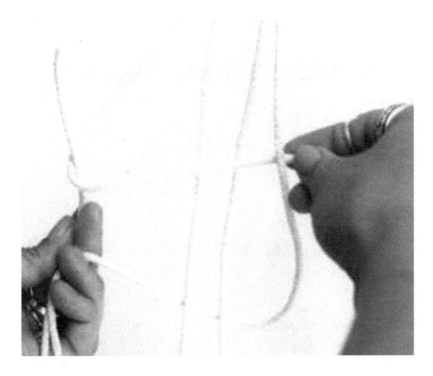

Tighten the loop by pulling the outer strands together and start with the left to repeat the process on the four strands. You will then see that a square knot has formed after tightening the loops together.

Connect the strands together by doing square knots with the remaining four pieces of rope and then repeat the process again from the left side. Tighten the loop by pulling the outer strands together and start with the left to repeat the process on the four strands. You will then see that a square knot has formed after loops have been tightened together.

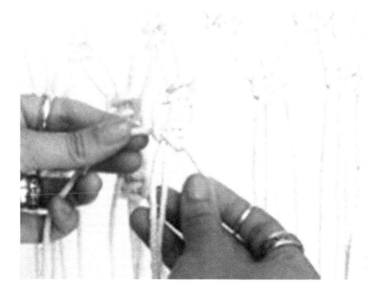

You can then do an eight knot and then just attach charms and feathers to the end. Glue them in and burn the ends for better effect!

## Wreath of Nature

Just imagine having a Macramé wreath in your home! This one is inspired by nature and is one of the most creative things you could do with your time!

What you need:

Clips or tape

Fabric glue

Wreath or ring frame

80 yards 12" cords

160 yards 17-18" cords

140 yards 14-16" cords

120 yards 12-13" cords

Instructions:

Mount the cords on top of the wreath and make the crown knot by folding one of the cords in half. Let the cords pass through the ring and then fold a knot and make sure to place it in front of the ring. Let the loops go over the ring and pull them your way so they could pass the area that has been folded.

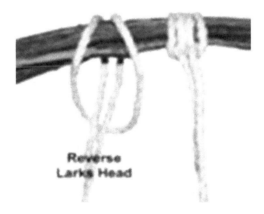

Let the ends pass over the first loop so you could make way for some half-hitches. Let them go over and under the ring, and then tightly pull it over the cord. This way, you'd get something like the one below. Repeat these first few steps until you have mounted all the cords on top of the ring. Organize them in groups of ten.

Now, you can make leaf-like patterns. To do this, make sure to number the first group of cords on the right side and make half-hitches in a counter-clockwise direction. Take note that you have to place the holding plate horizontally. If you see that it has curved slightly, make sure to reposition it and then attach cords labeled 5 to 7. Move it to resemble a diagonal position and then attach cords 8 to 10.

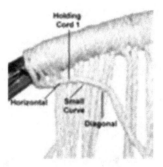

Make sure knots have been pushed close together and then use the cord on the leftmost corner to lower the leaf-like portion. The first four cords should be together on the handle and then go and attach cords labeled 3 to 6 to the holding cord. Move the cords so they'd be in a horizontal position.

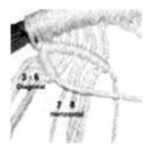

Now, move the cord upwards so that the center would not curve unnecessarily. Repeat the process for the cords on the bottom part of the frame and then start making the branches by selecting 2 to 4 cords from each of the leaves. Don't select the first and second row's first and last leaves.

Hold the cords with tape or clips as you move them towards the back of the design and decide how you want to separate—or keep the branches together. Secure the cords with glue after moving them to the back.

Wrap the right cords around the ones on the left so that branches could be joined together. Make sure to use half-hitches to wrap this portion and then use a set of two cords to create a branch.

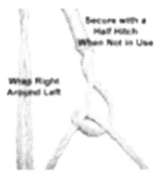

Together with your wrap, make use of another wrap and make sure they all come together as one.

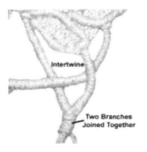

Secure the bundle by wrapping a 3-inch wrap cord around it and then let it go over the completed knot.

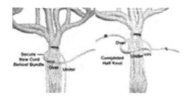

As for the fringe, you have to divide the knots into groups of two and make sure to tie a half-hitch on the rightmost cord on the left, and then let them alternate back and forth continuously under you have managed to cover your whole wreath. Let each sent slide under the whole wreath and then attach each cord to the ring itself.

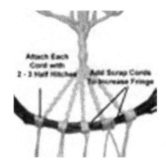

Make sure to divide the cords into small groups and then use the cords so you could tie the overhand knots. Unravel the fibers so you could form a wavy fringe.

That's it! You now have your own Macramé Wreath of Nature!

# CHAPTER 9:

# Unique Ideas Also For Kids With Fun Projects And Patterns (Outstanding, Beautiful Do-It-Yourself Projects For Macramé That Even Kids Can Make)

## Macramé Skirt Hanger

**What you need:**

12 mm size beads

One 8-inch ring

One 2-inch ring

4mm cord

Instructions:

Cut 8 cords that are at least 8.5 yards long then cut a cord that is 36 inches long before cutting 4 more yards of cord.

Fold the 8.5 yard in half to start the top part of the thread. Let it pass through the ring and let some parts drape down before choosing two cords from outside the bundle. Make sure to match the ends and then try the square knot.

You should find the center and move 8 inches down from it and then stop when you reach 12 inches.

Wrap the center a couple of times and then pull the ends tightly until you build a sturdy bundle, and then tug on the ends so that the roll could get smaller.

Make a total of four spirals that could at least be 20 inches and then manage the filler cords by adding a bead to them.

Attach the cords to the 8-inch ring by using double half-hitch stitches and then arrange the cords so they could be in four groups. Pull the stitches tightly so there is enough spacing and then mount all the cords to the ring in counterclockwise motion. To cover the ring, make sure to tie a half-hitch at each end.

Make alternating square knots just below the ring and divide into two groups of 40 strings each—it sounds like a lot, but it is what would naturally happen. Add some tape to the cords you have labeled 1 to 40 and then tie a half-square knot to the four injected threads. Add some beads, and then tie a knot again.

Add beads to cords 20 to 21 after using cords 19 to 22 and then make alternating square knots and then repeat on the cords on the back side. Add beads and make more alternating square knots, then add beads to cords 16 to 17 after using cords labeled 15 to 18. Tie the next row without adding any beads and then use cords 11 to 30. Work on cords 12 to 29 by adding beads to them and making use of alternating square knots. Repeat the 3rd row with no beads, and the 4th row with beads and choose four of your favorite cords to make fringes.

## Macramé Speaker Hanger

**What you need:**

Measuring tape

Fabric glue

Brass rings

50 yards paracord

Instructions:

Cut 16 cords that are 15 yards long, then cut 2 cords that are 2 yards long, and finally, cut 2 cords that are 60 inches long.

What you must do is wrap the two rings together using 2 cords and by tying with the crown knot. Make use of half hitch stitches to secure the wrap and then find the center of the cord. Make sure to secure them on the surface and to hold them close together. 8 of the two cords should then be lined up in a central manner so that they would be able to hold the speaker.

Now, go and bundle the long cords by wrapping and pulling them tightly together and letting the first end pass under the last coil. Wrap securely so it would not unravel.

Make sure to pull more cords from the bundles and then tighten the wraps on the center with your working cords. Let the lower portion come together by using square knots and make sure that you go and tighten the first half of it. Tie the second half around the board and then turn the board around after you have let the rolled coils pass through at one end of the ring.

Use half-hitches to arrange the center and let the rolled bundles dangle on the other end of the ring. Fold the sennit so you could match it with the last couple of knots, and then wrap the scrap cord around it. Now, put the hanger horizontally on your workspace and secure with square knots.

Let the working end pass through the middle of the bundle and then bring the working end around the bundle that you are using. Let it pass over the front and under the cord's back and keep wrapping as firmly as you can until you see something that looks like a loop.

Take the pin away from the secured end and pull until you reach the knot inside. Make use of fabric glue to coat this with and trim the ends. Let flame pass through it to secure it, as well.

Tie 5 half knots to keep the hanger secure and start suspending on the wall or ceiling—whichever you prefer. Place some beads before tying the knot again, and then make use of fillers as working cords before firmly tightening the knot. Create 25 more square knots and push the knots up to eliminate spooling. Repeat process until your desired length.

Finally, make a figure-eight knot and make sure to pull the end tightly before tying several more.

## Macramé Tie-Dye Necklace

This one is knotted tightly, which gives it the effect that it is strong—but still elegant. This is a good project to craft—you would enjoy the act of making it, and wearing it, as well!

**What you need:**

1 pack laundry rope

Tulip One-Step Dye

Fabric glue

Candle

Jump rings

Lobster clasp

Instructions:

Tie the rope using crown knots

After tying, place the knotted rope inside the One-Step Dye pack (you could get this in most stores) and let it set and dry overnight.

Upon taking it out, leave it for a few hours and then secure the end of the knot with fabric glue mixed with a bit of water.

Trim the ends off and burn off the ends with wax from candle.

Add jump rings to the end and secure with lobster clasp.

Enjoy your tie-dye necklace!

## Macramé Watch Strand

If you are looking for ways to spice up your wristwatch, well, now's your chance! Make use of this Macramé Watch Strand Pattern and you will get what you want!

**What you need:**

Jump rings

Closure

2mm Crimp ends (you can choose another size, depending on your preferences)

Embroidery or craft floss

Watch with posts

Instructions:

Choose your types of floss, as well as their colors. Take at least 10 long strands for each side of the watch.

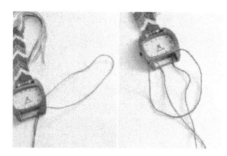

Lash each floss onto the bar/posts of the watch and thread like you would a regular Macramé bracelet or necklace.

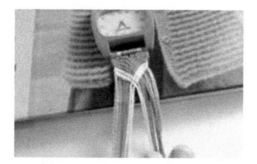

Braid the ends tightly if you want to make it more stylish and cut the ends. Burn with lighter to secure before placing jump rings and closure.

Use and enjoy!

CHAPTER 10:

# Instruction Books

Learn macramé with step by step instructions accompanied by real knot pictures.

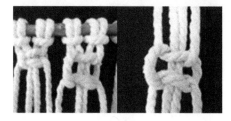

## Plant Hanger Ayla

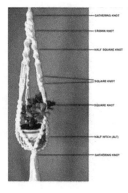

Description: Plant hanger of 2 feet and 3,5 inches (70 cm)

Used Knots: Square knot, half square knot, alternating square knot, crown knot, gathering knot, and half hitch knot

Supplies: 4 strands of a cord of 13 feet and 1,5 inches (4 meters), 4 strands of 16 feet and 4,8 inches (5 meters), 2 strands of 3 feet and 3,4 inches (1 meter), 1 wooden ring of 2 inches (50 mm) and 4 wooden beads: diameter 0,4 inches (10mm)

Directions (step-by-step):

1. Fold the 8 longer strands of cord in half through the wooden ring. Tie all (now 16) strands together with 1 shorter strand of 3 feet and 3,4 inches (1 m) with a gathering knot. Cut the cord ends off after tying the gathering knot.

2. Now follows the crown knot. It is the easiest when you turn your project up-side-down in between your legs, as shown in the photos. Divide the 16 strands into 4 sets of 4 strands each. Each set has 2 long strands and 2 shorter strands. Tie 5 crown knots in each set. Pull each strand tight and smooth.

3. Tie 15 half square knots on each set of four strands. In each set, the 2 shorter strands are in the middle and you are tying with the 2 outer, longer strands. Dropdown 2,4 inches (6 cm of no knots).

4. Tie 1 square knot with each set.

5. Then add the wooden bead to the 2 inner cords of each set and tie 1 square knot with each set again. Dropdown 2,4 inches (6 cm of no knots) and tie 6 square knots with each of the 4 sets.

6. Take 2 strands of 1 set and make 10 alternating half hitch knots. Repeat for the 2 left strands of that set. And then repeat for all sets.

7. Tie an alternating square knot to connect the left two cords in each set with the right two of the set next to it. Followed by 3 square knots for each new set (so you have 4 square knots in total for each new-formed set).

8. Place your chosen container/bowl into the hanger to make sure it will fit, gather all strands together and then tie a gathering knot with the left-over shorter strand of 3 feet and 3,4 inches (1 m). Trim all strands to the length that you want. If you want you can unravel the ends of each strand.

## Plant Hanger Bella

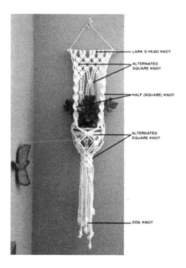

Description: Plant hanger of 60 cm (not counting the fringe)

Supplies: 6 strands of the cord of 13 feet and 1,5 inches (4 meters), 4 strands of 16 feet and 4,8 inches (5 meters) and a wooden stick of 11,8 inches (30cm)

Used Knots: A half knot, Lark´s Head knot, (Alternating) square knot and Coil knot

Directions (step-by-step):

1. Fold all strands in half and tie them to the wooden stick with Lark´s Head knot. The longest strands are on the outer side (2 strands at the left side and 2 at the right).

2. Make 4 rows of alternating square knots. (See knot guide for explanation)

3. In the 5th row, you only make 2 alternating square knots on the right and 2 on the left.

4. In the 6th row, you only tie 1 alternating square on each side.

5. Then, with the 4 strands on the side, you tie 25 half (square) knots. Do this for both sides, the left and right sides.

6. Take 4 strands from the middle of the plant hanger, first drop down 2,4 inches (6 cm of no knots) and then tie a square knot with the 4 center strands. Now with the 4 strands next to the middle, drop down 3,15 inches (8 cm of no knots), and tie a square knot. Do this for both sides (left and right).

7. Dropdown 2,4 inches (6 cm of no knots) and tie 2 (alternated) square knots by taking 2 strands from both sides (right and left group). Then 3 alternating square knots with the other groups. These knots must be about at the same height where the strands with the half knots have ended.

8. Take the 2 outer strands of the left group, which you made 25 half knots, and take the 2 outer strands of the group on the right. First dropping down 2,4 inches (6 cm of no knots), you tie a square knot with these 4 strands.

9. Do the same with the rest of the strands leftover, make groups of 4 strands and tie alternated square knots on the same height as the one you made in step 8. Dropdown 2,4 inches (6 cm of no knots) and make another row of alternated square knots using all strands.

10. Dropdown 2,4 inches (6 cm of no knots) and make 5 rows of alternated square knots. Be careful: this time leave NO space in between the alternated square knots and you make them as tight as possible.

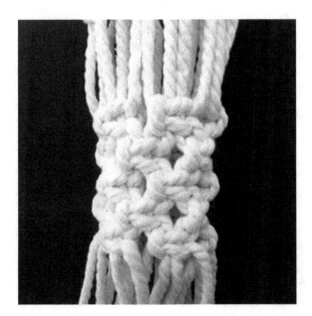

11. Dropdown as many inches/cm as you want to make the fringe and tie at all ends a coiled knot.

12. Then cut off all strands, directly under each coil knot.

## Plant Hanger Cathy

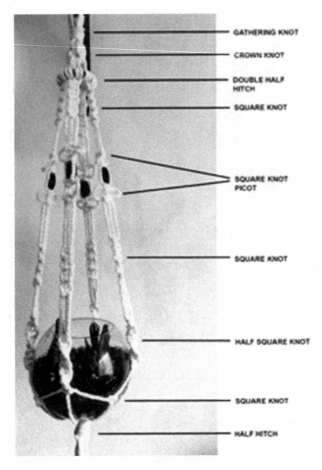

Description: Plant hanger of 2 feet and 9,5 inches (85 cm) - not counting the fringe

Supplies: 4 wooden beads of 1,2 inches (3cm), 3 inches (7,5cm) wooden ring, 4 cords of 18 feet (5,5 meter), 2 cords of 15 feet (4,5 meter) and 1 cord of 2 feet and 1,6 inches (65 centimeters)

Used Knots: Gathering knot, crown knot, (double) half hitch, (Half) square knot and Square knot

Directions (step-by-step):

1. Fold the 6 longer cords in half, placing the loops neatly side by side. Use a gathering knot for tying the cords together with the shortest cord. This gives you twelve cords in total.

2. Arrange the cords in four groups of three cords each. Make sure that each group consists out of 2 longer cords and 1 shorter cord. Tie three Chinese Crown knots with the four groups of cords.

3. Slip the wooden ring over the top loop and drop it down 1,2 inches (3 cm) from the last Chinese Crown knot. With each of the twelve cords, tie one double half hitch on the ring to secure it. This gives you a ring of double half hitches.

4. Arrange the cords into four groups of three cords each. The middle cord of each group is the shorter one, this is called the filler cord. Repeat step five thru eight for each group.

5. Tie four square knots, each having one shorter, filler cord.

6. Skip down 2 inches (5 cm). Tie one square knot picot.

7. Slide a bead up the filler cord. Tie another square knot picot directly under the bead.

8. Skip down 2 inches (5 cm). Tie five square knots, each having one filler cord.

9. Skip down 2 inches (5 cm). Tie 10 half square knots, each having one filler cord.

10. Repeat the following procedure for each of the four groups you have just knotted: skip down 2,4 inches (6 cm); take one cord from each neighboring square knot to tie a square knot WITHOUT a filler cord. This gives you four square knots made of two cords each. The cords in the middle of each group are NOT used to knot.

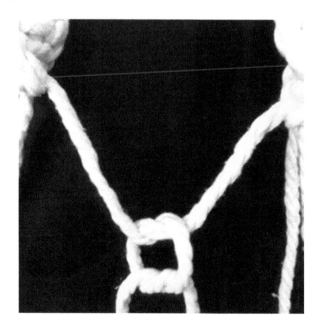

11. Skip down 4,8 inches (12 cm). Gather and tie all cords together with one of cords hanging using to tie 10 times a half hitch.

12. Cut the fringe to measure 6 inches (15 cm).

CHAPTER 11:

# The Most Effective Method To Macramé

For individuals who might want to figure out how to Macramé, there are many places accessible. Creating complicated knots that make total examples that can additionally be changed into beautiful bracelets, flower boxes, and decorative wall hangings are what Macramé is focused on as art. The first and least confounded stage in attempting to figure out how to Macramé, in case you're keen on this theme, is understanding the essential knots and a couple of diagrams.

The internet is a decent place to start searching for a way to figure out how to Macramé. Visual guides are of monstrous help and will make figuring out how to macramé hassle-free. For loads of people, it is significantly simpler to follow diagrams rather than written directions that can be extremely hard to comprehend. Also, when you have acclimated yourself with the visual guides, the time has come to get the provisions to begin the procedure of Macramé.

Looking at a diagram, paying little mind to how well exhaustive and clarified it is, won't offer a lot of help for you to have the option to Macramé appropriately. It's essential to have the string to have the opportunity to Macramé productively necessarily. Like with any procured art, attempting to figure out how to Macramé additionally includes practice. Get some unmistakable, preparing portrayals of basic diagrams to get started. You'll see the less complex ones as less complicated than the complexities of the modern ones. You'll have the option to advance into them with a lot of time and exercise.

Besides the basic knot designs, you will likewise have the option to center and practice for a little before you can remember the activities and make symmetrical knots. This won't be educated if you're in a rush and need to make things stride by step to figure out how to Macramé. When you've culminated, the major knot structures, at that point, continue to arrange them to make essential works, for example, bracelets. Besides the knots, you likewise need to have an eye to coordinate the best colorings to draw out the knot works.

Wristbands are fantastic for beginners as the most straightforward knots are required without a high level of intricacy. At the point when you feel increasingly sure with your ability, you can handle extremely excellent examples. The best positive concerning mind-boggling and exceptionally confounded plans is that they can only be formed to deliver elaborate things that show up unprecedented.

To decide a timeframe that will take to figure out how to Macramé will rely upon various factors like how rapidly you can learn the strategy. Should you have been knitting or sewing for quite a while, the complexity level ought to be fundamentally less since there are a few likenesses with the technique.

## Amateur Macramé

Much the same as anything in life, there is an endless number of ways of learning another skill or craft. I won't profess to be a specialist in Macramé. I am a total beginner. Starting with one beginner then onto the next, I am just going to take you through my journey to give you one way to do it.

I will give all the assets you have to locate your specific manner to grasp the pleasant specialty of Macramé. The cool part is that you don't should be a specialist to make wonderful stylistic layout pieces for your home. Truly, it looks a lot harder than it is. In this way, how about we get to it.

## First: Practice How To Do Macramé

For what reason would it be advisable for you to practice first? Like most anything, this project is going to cost you a bit. What amount? My first 'genuine' project cost me about $30 for the macramé cord (or macramé line, as it is at times alluded to) and several dollars for the wooden dowel.

Moreover, you can't get down to Hobby Lobby or Michael's and purchase the macramé cord or macramé cord. You will need to arrange it (more on that later). In case you're similar to me, and you like to begin a project the day you, at last, say to yourself, "I need to begin this," I propose to start as I did with a training project.

I looked on YouTube for "Simple Macramé Tutorial" and presto, I began my first smaller than expected project. There are knots of amateur macramé projects and instructional exercises on YouTube.

CHAPTER 12:

# Modern macramé

My age missed the 70's, and that is unquestionably alright. It means, however, that I passed up certain things. Things like bellbottoms, afros, bordered coats, and macramé. If you are a millennial (might I venture to try and use that word?), you may never have at any point known about macramé.

You and I are in a comparable situation. A year back, somebody was portraying makes that were in-style, and they raised macramé. I claimed to comprehend what they were discussing until I couldn't anymore. I, in the end, needed to concede my numbness. "What is macramé?"

Macramé is essentially the specialty of ornamental knot tying. Merriam Webster characterizes it as: "A coarse ribbon or periphery made by knotting strings or lines in a geometrical example; likewise, the specialty of tying knots in patterns." If you look into pictures, you will see tons of divider designs and plant holders that have a lacy look to them.

Growing up, I had just, at any point, seen macramé as a plant holder in my grandma's front room and was under the impression that it was a much more seasoned style. It turns out; the plant holder was not my grandma's doing but my dad's.

In addition to the fact that I thought that macramé was from my grandma's age, I likewise thought it was an art, for the most part, practiced by ladies. The bordered coats of the past, and the to a great extent female creating a segment on Pinterest today gave me an inappropriate thought. Since getting taught on macramé, I have found that many middle-aged men I realize today were into macramé, thinking back to the '70s.

## Macramé Demystified

It turns out I definitely knew how to macramé, and you most likely do as well. If you make paracord armbands, you know macramé. Similar knots are utilized in both. On the off chance that you think the cobra weave armband was a military thing, think once more. Macramé is, for the most part, comprised of square knots, which are, at any rate, 4,000 years of age, presumably a lot more established. At some point over the last 20 years, a man stated, "I can't wear macramé. How about we call it something extreme? What about 'Cobra'? That sounds intense."

Thus the paracord "cobra" armband was conceived. It turns out this was just a modern twist on something that had been around for quite a while.

## More Than You Need to Know

I covered quite a bit of this in A Selective History of Knots and Rope, however, here's a snappy history of macramé:

- 1200's Arab weavers started utilizing knots to decorate the edges of materials. This style relocated to Spain under Moorish impact.

- Late 1600's Macramé was brought into the English court of Mary II.

- Mid 1800's British and American mariners practiced knot work while at sea and traded them at ports the world over.

- 1800's Macramé became well known in material frivolity and home stylistic theme, somewhat becoming outdated when the new century rolled over.

- 1970's Macramé had a resurgence during the "hippy years" as an approach to decorating, just as having beneficial uses, for example, plant holders or tablecloths.

- The 2010s After only around 20-30 years of unpopularity, macramé is, by and by well, known as a component of the boho hippy style.

## Macramé Today

The macramé of today has a refreshed shading palette. Except if somebody is purposefully duplicating the 70's to coordinate their retro shag cover, it's typically made of each shading in turn, generally white, pastels, or earth tones. In any case, that is not so reasonable; macramé can be made in a wide range of styles. It's mostly beautiful knot work.

As a store that sells different sorts of creating rope, we at Paracord Planet are a little astounded when individuals look at our site for "macramé line." Traditionally, cotton and hemp rope was generally healthy. However, those were only the ropes of their time anything goes.

In its latest rebound, manufactured filaments are frequently utilized, even paracord. Other macramé strings incorporate cotton rope, engineered to create a chain, manila/hemp rope, jute, and even calfskin. Any cable can be a macramé rope. I'm sure some time or another, the cutting edge will take a gander at modern macramé and regard it as extraordinarily obsolete and wonder how we could believe that something so ugly was ever lovely, much the same as we did to our folks.

It's easy to begin in macramé. It's a broad classification of creating, so anybody can discover something in the pastime that accommodates their style. To begin, here are two macramé instructional exercises that we as of late put out.

CHAPTER 13:

# Table Runner

All you need to know is three essential nodes, and you have a charming layer that works every season. If you know the knots learned here, you can tailor your table runner to the length of your table or change it totally and create a hanging macramé wall.

**Supply:** -12" wooden dowel –22 lengths of cotton rope measuring 3 mm –with cotton twine over the door–2" with dowel hanger scissors

- **Step 1:**

Apply cotton twine to each end of the dowel and hang it on the door hanger. Fold your first 16" rope strand in half and create a knot on your dowel. For even more thorough measures, see this article.

- **Step 2:**

Use the same beach to tie a second knot to the foundation line. This is regarded as a halving knot.

- **Step 3:**

Make sure they are clear and even.

- **Step 4:**

Repeat from the outside with the second, third and fourth ropes and tie another hitch-knot, so it is snug, etc. You're going to begin to see the trend. It's a half-hitch horizontal.

- **Step 5:**

Continue to tie successive cords throughout a single knot. You don't want to be so close that it's at the edges in the distance.

- **Step 6:**

From the right again, use the four outer strands to build a knot about 1.5" below the horizontal knots. See this macramé storage article for more information on a square knot. Out the four (five to eight) strands then tie another knot of nine to twelve strands. Keep skipping four before you cross the line.

- **Step 7:**

begin again on the right, use the four strands that you skipped (five to eight) and tie a square knot about 3" below the dowel.

- **Step 8:**

Continue tying four-strand sets in square knots until the row is ended.

horizontal knots. Then use the following four strands to create another 1.5" square knot over the last square knot.

- **Step 9:**

Start as shown. You're not going to do anything with the last two lines.

- **Step 10:**

Going back from the right, build another series of half-hitch horizontal knot by repeating steps 3 through 7.

- **Step 11:**

From the left side, use the same base rope string and produce horizontal half-hitch of knots about 2.5" below. You're going to work on this from left to right.

- **Step 12:**

Starting from the left side, create a row of knots without skipping any threads that are roughly 1" below that line of knots. Instead, create a second row of the quadratic knot, miss the first two threads on the left, and tie a full line of quadratic knots. This is known as an alternating knot. You don't want much space between these rows so you can draw them closer together as each square node is inserted.

- **Step 13:**

Keep going until you have a total of approximately 13 rows of alternating knots. This segment is the core of your table runner so that everything else will represent what has already been woven above.

- **Step 14:**

Add another half-hitch horizontal knot from the outside left and work on the right.

- **Step 15:**

Downward nearly 2.5" and use the same base rope to create another horizontal half-hitch tie from the right to the right.

- **Step 16:**

Skip two outer strands of rope to the right for this segment and tie a square knot with strands three to six. Slip seven to 10 strands and use 11 to 14 strands to tie another knot. Repeat so that every four strands you missed. On the left, you're going to have six strands.

Turn one, and two rows left and tie three to six threads to a square knot around 1.5" underneath that last row of square knots. Then miss the four strands for the second row of square nodes and complete the sequence. This will leave you on the right side with six extra threads.

- **Step 17:**

Measure 11" from the last row of horizontal ties and tie a knot of the square by using the four outside strands to the right. Then tie the four in a square knot about 1.5" above the last knot.

## Step 18: Repeat throughout.

Take note of how long the ends are on the other side as long as you like. Cut the twine of the cotton from your dowel and loosen all the knots of the lark carefully. Then cut the middle of the head of the lark and remove the sides.

You are now ready to set a charming table!

The middle of your dining table is the ideal place to put a centerpiece, so lie on a trivet, and you can find fresh flowers to anchor your hand. You can even use it as your giant cupboard in a breakfast bar, to make sure your kitchen looks best! You can also use the three common knots, the knot of the lark, the knot of half-hitch and the knot of the square to create a set of textured hanging walls!

Do you need something more colored? Use these stunning 3 mm and 5 mm Custom Macramé colored lines.

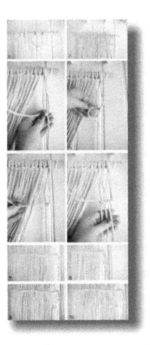
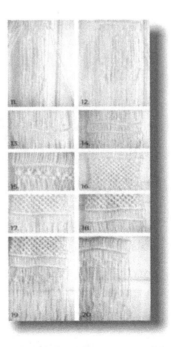

# Conclusion

The beauty of Macramé as a vintage art that has survived extinction for centuries and has continued to thrive as a technique of choice for making simple but sophisticated items is simply unrivalled. The simple fact that you have decided to read this manual means that you are well on your way to making something great. There is truly a certain, unequaled feeling of satisfaction that comes from crafting your own masterpiece, and by reading this book, you have taken the first step towards experiencing that feeling of euphoria.

Macramé can also serve as an avenue for you to begin your dream small business. After perfecting your Macramé skills, you can conveniently sell your items and get paid well for your products, especially if you can perfectly make items like bracelets that people buy a lot. You could even train people and start your own little company that makes bespoke Macramé fashion accessories. The opportunities that Macramé presents are truly endless.

As you have read this book, do not simply discard it. Keep it as a guide, and look out for more extensive materials online and offline to help you perfect your skills. This book explains basic knots and projects for beginners, but if you practice Macramé regularly, you wouldn't be a beginner for long. As stated earlier, Macramé can be very relaxing, and it is an amazing avenue to bring family and friends together. As you have learnt here, you can teach your loved ones some of these basic knots, and refer them to obtain their copy of this carefully prepared beginner's guide to Macramé.

The most important rule in Macramé is the maxim: "Practice makes perfect." If you cease to practice constantly, your skills are likely to deteriorate over time. So keep your skills sharp, exercise the creative parts of your brain, and keep creating mind-blowing handmade masterpieces. Jewelry and fashion accessories made with even the most basic Macramé knots are always a beauty to behold, hence they serve as perfect gifts for loved ones on special occasions. Presenting a Macramé bracelet to someone, for instance passes the message that you didn't just remember to get them a gift, you also treasure them so much that you chose to invest your time into crafting something unique specially for them too, and trust me, that is a very powerful message. However, the most beautiful thing about Macramé is perhaps the fact that it helps to create durable items. Hence you can keep a piece of decoration, or a fashion accessory you made for yourself for many years, enjoy the value and still feel nostalgic anytime you remember when you made it. It even feels better when you made that item with someone. This feature of durability also makes Macramé accessories incredibly perfect gifts.

Macramé can also serve as an avenue for you to begin your dream small business. After perfecting your Macramé skills, you can conveniently sell your items and get paid well for your products, especially if you can perfectly make items like bracelets that people buy a lot. You could even train people and start your own little company that makes bespoke Macramé fashion accessories. The opportunities that Macramé presents are truly endless.

So stay sharp, keep practicing and keep getting better. Welcome to a world of infinite possibilities!

CPSIA information can be obtained
at www.ICGtesting.com
Printed in the USA
LVHW060749230221
679511LV00012B/66